MT. DENALI

(MCKINLEY) - UNITED STATES (ALASKA)
HEIGHT: 20,310 FEET / 6,190 METERS

MT. ACONCAGUA

ARGENTINA / HEIGHT: 22,840 FEET / 6,962 METERS

MT. ELBRUS

RUSSIA / HEIGHT: 18,510 FEET / 5,642 METERS

MT. EVEREST

NEPAL/TIBET
HEIGHT: 29,032 FEET / 8,849 METERS

THE SEVEN SUMMITS

These mountains represent the highest peaks on each of the seven continents. Climbing all seven is a major goal for mountaineers worldwide.

MT. KILIMANJARO

TANZANIA / HEIGHT: 19,341 FEET / 5,895 METERS

MT. KOSCIUSZKO

AUSTRALIA (MAINLAND)
HEIGHT: 7,310 FEET / 2,228 METERS

MT. VINSON

ANTARCTICA / HEIGHT: 16,050 FEET / 4,892 METERS

THE SEVEN SUMMITS

MOUNT VINSON

SARA GILBERT

CREATIVE EDUCATION • CREATIVE PAPERBACKS

Published by Creative Education and Creative Paperbacks
P.O. Box 227, Mankato, Minnesota 56002
Creative Education and Creative Paperbacks
are imprints of The Creative Company
www.thecreativecompany.us

Design by Graham Morgan
Art direction by Blue Design (www.bluedes.com)

Images by Alamy Stock Photo/Cavan Images, 2, DOD Photo, 9, 35; Dreamstime/Aleksandra Alekseeva, 28, Cristian Tecu, 32, Extezy, cover, 1, Igor Dmitriev, 25, Mogens Trolle, 17, Mrotchua, 30, Pecorb, 1, Vladislav Zhukov, 26; Getty Images/STR, 22; Public Domain, 18; Shutterstock/lusia83, 43; Wikimedia Commons/Chic500, 41, Christian R. Rohleder, 16, Christopher Michel, 6, 24, Christian Stangl, 45, Cmichel67, 31, Dave Pape, 14–15, Harris & Ewing, 13, Hugh Broughton Architects, 23, Kirschi165, 29, NASA, 38–39, NASA/Michael Studinger, 37, Nasjonalbiblioteket, 21, Paul Berge, 10, public domain, 20, 40, public domain/Daniel Georg Nyblin, 33, public domain/Yellowstone National Park, 36, United States Department of the Interior: Geological Survey, 4–5

Library of Congress Cataloging-in-Publication Data
Names: Gilbert, Sara, author.
Title: Mount Vinson / Sara Gilbert.
Description: Mankato, Minnesota : Creative Education, Creative Paperbacks, 2025. | Series: The seven summits | Includes bibliographical references and index. | Audience: Ages 10–14 | Audience: Grades 4–6 | Summary: "Mount Vinson is Antarctica's tallest peak and a Seven Summits mountaineering challenge. This guide for kids age 12 and up examines the mountain's geologic and climbing history. Includes a glossary, sidebars, profiles of notable climbers, and further resources"—Provided by publisher.
Identifiers: LCCN 2024023451 (print) | LCCN 2024023452 (ebook) | ISBN 9798889892755 (library binding) | ISBN 9781682776414 (paperback) | ISBN 9798889893868 (ebook)
Subjects: LCSH: Mountaineering—Antarctica—Vinson Massif—Juvenile literature. | Vinson Massif (Antarctica)—Juvenile literature.
Classification: LCC GV199.44.A6 G55 2025 (print) | LCC GV199.44.A6 (ebook) | DDC 796.52209989—dc23/eng/20240610
LC record available at https://lccn.loc.gov/2024023451
LC ebook record available at https://lccn.loc.gov/2024023452

Printed in the United States of America

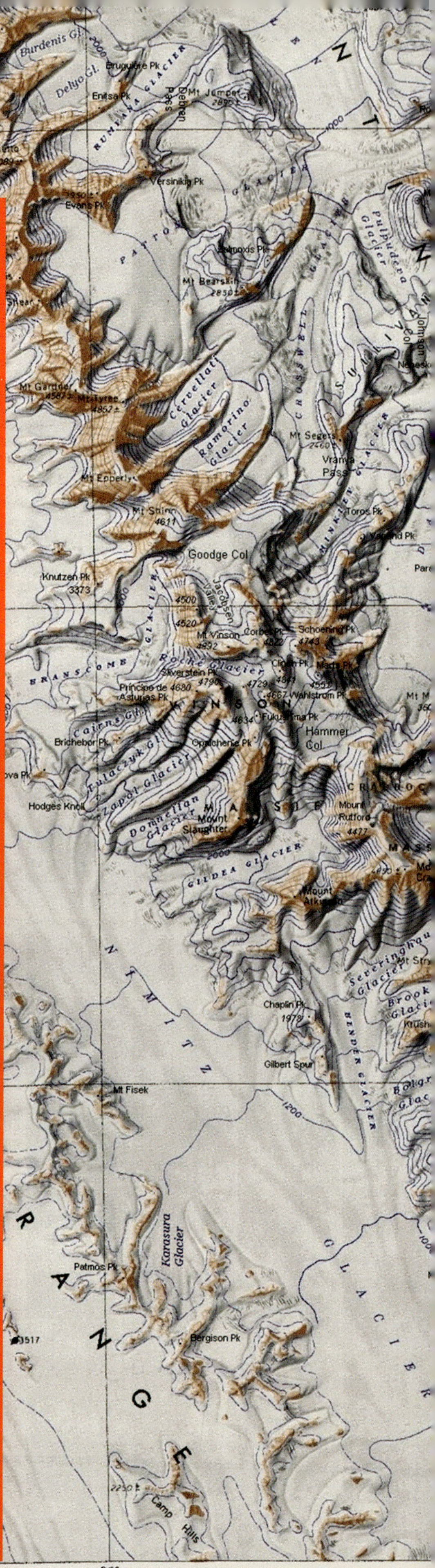

0,000

INTERIOR—GEOLOGICAL SURVEY, RESTON, VIRGINIA—1989

Visitors to Antarctica's Mount Vinson region may sleep in the clamshell tents of Union Glacier Camp.

CONTENTS

INTRODUCTION

Although each of the seven continents on Earth varies greatly in terms of climate, geography, culture, and economic engines, they all share a few common elements. One of those is that they all have at least one mountain range and, within that range, a tallest peak. Together, those peaks are known as the **Seven Summits**.

Reaching the top of all seven peaks is a challenge that mountain climbers have strived to achieve for decades. It is not an easy feat. The first person to successfully complete it was Richard Bass in 1985. Since then, only about 500 other climbers have reached the elusive goal. Many others have tried, but due to a variety of challenges—from finances to technical difficulties—the club still remains exclusive.

Towering over Antarctica, Mount Vinson was the last of the Seven Summits to be discovered. For those ambitious climbers seeking to join the Seven Summits Club, it is usually one of the last to be climbed—not because of its difficulty but because of its remote location. Only about 1,400 climbers have made it to the top of Mount Vinson since it was first summited in 1966.

Climbers near Mount Vinson's summit have a view of the rugged Ellsworth Mountains.

In addition to his trans-Antarctic air crossing, Lincoln Ellsworth also flew over the North Pole in 1926.

CHAPTER 1: ICY RANGE

In 1935, explorer Lincoln Ellsworth attempted the first cross-continent flight of Antarctica. While in the air, he and his pilot, Herbert Hollick-Kenyon, caught a glimpse of a spectacular mountain range rising from the icy landscape. The sight took their breath away. But before they could get close enough to explore more, their airplane ran out of fuel, forcing an emergency landing. Ellsworth called the mountains he had seen the Sentinel Range. Later, the chain of mountains to which the Sentinel Range belongs was named the Ellsworth Mountains, in honor of the man who discovered them.

The Ellsworth Mountains, which are located on the western edge of the Ronne Ice Shelf, are very difficult to explore. They stretch 224 miles (360 kilometers) across western Antarctica, running from north to south. The massive Minnesota Glacier separates the Sentinel Range in the north from the Heritage Range in the south. The mountains are so remote and difficult to get to that, following Ellsworth's glimpse, almost 25 years passed before a U.S. Navy pilot, flying on a military observation mission in 1957, took note of one particular peak towering above the others. That peak was the highest of several in a distinct mountain mass known as a **massif**. It was the first time anyone had seen Mount Vinson, the highest peak in Antarctica.

Following the sighting, scientists used the best tools available at the time to measure the mountain's height. They set it at 16,964 feet (5,140 meters). But as tools for measuring became more sophisticated, and as climbers were actually able to reach the summit, more accurate measurements were collected. In 2001, a team of climbers took **global positioning system** measurements as they ascended the slopes. Their research led to a change in the official measurement of the mountain. Mount Vinson is now listed at 16,050 feet (4,892 m) above sea level.

Mount Vinson is part of the Vinson Massif, which is 13 miles (21 km) long and 8 miles (13 km) wide. The Vinson Massif includes eight separate peaks. Two of those peaks qualify as the second and third highest points on Antarctica: Mount Tyree, at 15,919 feet (4,852 m) and Mount Shinn, at 15,292 feet (4,661 m). Mount Vinson was likely formed along with the rest of the Ellsworth Mountains about 180 million years ago, after the **supercontinent** of Gondwanaland broke up. When forces inside Earth pushed the **tectonic plate** on which Antarctica sits upward and rotated it, the land was compressed and folded, creating the mountains that exist today.

Mount Vinson is composed of both **sedimentary** and volcanic rock. Its steeply inclined layers include three primary rock types: quartzite; fine, silty

ORIGINAL VINSON

Mount Vinson is named for a U.S. congressman from Georgia whose support of Antarctic exploration helped make its discovery possible. Carl G. Vinson served in the U.S. House of Representatives for more than 50 years, from 1914 until 1965. He championed Antarctic research explorations and helped strengthen the U.S. Navy. His name was given to both the Vinson Massif and the individual Mount Vinson peak—but those aren't his only namesakes. Vinson's long support of the U.S. Navy led to the naming of a nuclear-powered aircraft carrier in his honor, the USS *Carl Vinson*.

A satellite view of icy Antarctica

sedimentary deposits from the glaciers; and a layer of sandstone and argillite unique to Antarctica known as the Polarstar Formation.

Antarctica is also unique because it is almost entirely covered by the largest piece of ice in the world. The size of the Antarctic Ice Sheet varies depending on the time of year. In the summer, it is roughly 1.2 million square miles (3 million sq km). In the winter, it may be more than 7.3 million square miles (19 million sq km). That sheet of ice also covers the Ellsworth Mountains, including Mount Vinson.

All of that ice makes Mount Vinson an impossible place for animals and plants to live. Penguins, seals, orcas, whales, and many bird species thrive in the coastal areas of Antarctica. There they can feed on microscopic organisms called phytoplankton. But no animals live in the mountains, and the freezing temperatures

and poor soil quality limits the kinds of vegetation that can grow. Only three kinds of flowering plants exist on the continent. All of those are found only on the Antarctic Peninsula, where average temperatures are generally above freezing for at least one month of the year.

On Mount Vinson, the average temperature during the warmest months of the year—November through January, Antarctica's summer—is -20 degrees Fahrenheit (-30 degrees Celsius). Although the temperatures are always

Chunks of ice regularly break off Antarctica and float as icebergs in the open ocean.

Residents of Antarctica, Weddell seals are the world's southernmost breeding mammals.

extremely cold, the climate is relatively stable. On days when the wind is minimal and the sun is bright, it might even feel warm on the mountain. There is little precipitation, with annual snowfall averaging about 18 inches (46 centimeters) per year, but there can often be high winds at the lower levels of the mountain. That wind blows the snow around, which can impact visibility. Because of its nearness to the South Pole, Mount Vinson sees 24 hours of daylight during summer and no sunlight at all during the winter months (February through October).

The view from Mount Vinson is almost entirely white. The peak overlooks a series of snow-covered mountains and icy glaciers. Farther out, the Filchner-Ronne Ice Shelf is visible. It borders the Weddell Sea and leads into the Antarctic Peninsula. Farther still, where the land meets the sky, the curve of the Earth can be seen on the horizon. It is a stunning but barren landscape, one that very few people have had the opportunity to experience.

Early European explorers to Antarctica discovered a variety of new penguin species.

CHAPTER 2: LONELY LAND

Antarctica is the only continent on which there is no **indigenous** human population. Its extreme climate, icy terrain, and remote location have historically made it a difficult place for people to survive. But those same qualities—along with the search for oil, the hunt for seals, and the quest to conquer new land—have driven exploration of Antarctica for hundreds of years.

Oral histories suggest that Polynesian explorers may have sailed in Antarctic waters as early as the 7th century. The first European explorer to venture that far south was Captain James Cook, who recorded crossing into the Antarctic Circle in January 1773. Cook never sighted land. Fifty years later, both Russian and British captains reported seeing icy shores and snow-covered mountains. In 1823, Captain James Weddell navigated his ship farther south than anyone had before in search of seals. The Weddell Sea and the Weddell seals that live there were named for him.

The Heroic Age of Antarctic exploration began in 1899, when a British expedition spent the winter on the mainland and used dog sleds to explore the

area. Between 1901 and 1911, three separate crews attempted to reach the South Pole on land. The first to make it was Norwegian explorer Roald Amundsen, in December 1911. He was followed just a month later by Robert Falcon Scott, who died with the rest of his crew on the return trip. In 1921, famous explorer Sir Ernest Shackleton set off on an Antarctic expedition aboard a ship called *Quest*. Shackleton died on the ship just after reaching the islands that surround Antarctica. His crew tried to continued the voyage, but they were summoned back to England in June 1922 without accomplishing their goal.

Shackleton's failed trip ended the Heroic Age—but explorations of the frozen continent soon resumed with a renewed interest in conquering the land. Multiple countries laid claim to territories within Antarctica. By the 1940s, seven countries had claimed rights to sections of land on the continent: Argentina, Australia, Chile, France, New Zealand, Norway, and the United Kingdom. Some of those claims overlapped each other, and conflicts between countries arose. That led to an attempt to establish an international agreement, one that would preserve peace on the continent while encouraging a collaborative approach to the scientific research taking place there.

In 1959, 12 countries—the seven that had territorial claims, plus Belgium, Japan, South Africa, the Soviet Union, and the United States—signed the Antarctic Treaty. The agreement designated the continent as a scientific preserve. It also banned military activity on Antarctica. As of 2023, 56 countries had signed the treaty.

ROALD AMUNDSEN

RACE TO THE POLE

Antarctic exploration exploded in the early 20th century. The primary goal was to reach the South Pole. In 1911, British explorer Robert Falcon Scott and Norwegian explorer Roald Amundsen both set out to plant their country's flag at the pole. Amundsen, who had kept his mission secret, got a head start. His team set off from the Bay of Whales on October 18. The 60-mile (97-km) trek took almost two months, but on December 14, Amundsen planted Norway's flag at the South Pole. Scott didn't realize he had lost the race until he arrived there a month later, on January 17, 1912.

HEAVY METAL IN ANTARCTICA

Mountain climbers aren't the only people who set goals to visit all seven continents. So do rock bands! In 2013, the heavy-metal rock band Metallica achieved its goal of performing on all seven continents by hosting a concert from the Carlini Base, an Argentinian research station in Antarctica. Because of environmental protection laws that were enacted as part of the Antarctic Treaty, the band could not use traditional amplifiers during the performance. The audience of 120 people listened to the band through headphones.

The Halley Research Station, on an ice shelf in the Weddell Sea, is one of many facilities studying climate change and other global problems.

The Antarctic Treaty paved the way for greatly expanded scientific research. By 2023, 55 of the countries that had signed the treaty had established one or more research stations in Antarctica. There were 70 active research stations, some operating seasonally, others year-round, located across the continent. The people who work at those stations account for Antarctica's entire population. The total number varies throughout the year, but summer is the busiest time. More than 4,800 researchers and support staff live in Antarctica then. In the winter, when many of the stations close, the population dwindles to fewer than 1,200 people.

The closest research station to Mount Vinson is the Union Glacier Joint Scientific Polar Station, which was established in January 2014. The seasonal station is operated from November to January by the Chilean Antarctic Institute and the armed forces of Chile. It is located on Union Glacier, which is in the Ellsworth Mountain range. The scientists at that station research glacial changes and the effects of climate change on the environment, among other projects.

Antarctica is not considered a prime tourist destination. Getting there can be expensive, and the extreme conditions can be restrictive for some people.

Tents at Antarctica's Union Glacier Camp are heated naturally by summer's 24-hour sunlight.

EMPEROR PENGUIN

But it is a place that intrigues travelers, and private companies have created opportunities to explore the continent by air, land, or sea. Airplane tours are an option, although most do not land in Antarctica. Many people visit Antarctica on ocean cruises, which often include shore excursions as part of the package. Depending on where they dock, those excursions could include hiking, kayaking, or even snorkeling. Some travelers seek out the native penguins or look for whales. Tourists must have a permit through the Antarctic Treaty countries to land there.

Permits are also required of the adventurers and climbers who travel to the Ellsworth Mountains to test their strength and skill against the Antarctic extremes. Those visitors often arrive at the privately operated Union Glacier Camp, which is run by a company that leads expeditions in Antarctica. Jets can land on a naturally occurring blue ice runway. Some come from Russia, carrying supplies for the camp and people who work there. Charter flights from Chile also land there, carrying people ready to embark on an Antarctic adventure.

Some travelers fly in to Union Glacier to run the Antarctic Ice Marathon. Those extreme athletes run just over 26 miles (42 km) across the ice, only a few hundred miles from the South Pole. Some runners use the race as the first leg of the World Marathon Challenge, which includes seven marathons, one on each of the seven continents within seven days. Many people who arrive at Union Glacier Camp, however, arrive with a more lofty goal: to reach the summit of Mount Vinson.

Climbing walls provide good training for people wanting to tackle Mount Vinson.

CHAPTER 3: CLIMBING PREPARATIONS

The challenge of climbing Mount Vinson begins long before approaching the mountain. It is the most remote of the Seven Summits, and just getting to Antarctica to embark on the climb is an adventure in itself.

Before traveling to Antarctica, climbers should spend four to six months training for the physical and mental demands of the climb. Although Mount Vinson is classified as moderately difficult, climbers must be able to think clearly and quickly and be able to adapt to changing conditions. They must be in excellent physical shape to tackle the steep inclines, icy glaciers, and extreme weather. Climbing steep hills is the best way to prepare, but the ideal training program also includes exercises designed to build endurance, strength, balance, and flexibility.

Endurance training includes **cardiovascular** exercises such as running, biking, climbing hills, or running stairs—but with modifications to help prepare for mountain climbing. Carrying a weighted backpack and gradually adding additional weight helps, as most climbers carry up to 60 pounds (27 kilograms)

CLIMBING CARABINERS

in their packs to summit Mount Vinson. Increasing distance, speed, and intensity will also improve durability and prepare climbers for long days on the move.

Mountain climbing requires strong legs, a strong core (mid-body muscles), and a strong upper body. Strength training should include exercises that target all of those muscle groups, such as squats, lunges, push-ups, pull-ups, and sit-ups. Exercises that improve balance and **agility** are critical. Climbers need to have exceptional body awareness as they hike across uneven, icy, and unstable terrain. Standing on one leg, first with eyes open and then closed, and walking on a line or elevated rope can improve balance. Stretching is also important. It reduces tension and increases flexibility. It can also relax muscles strained by hard climbs and heavy backpacks. Stretching should involve every part of the body, including legs, arms, shoulders, back, and neck.

Almost as important as being physically fit for the climb is having the right gear and equipment. Mount Vinson is less than 700 miles (1,127 km) from the South Pole, which means climbers must be prepared for extremely cold temperatures. Sleeping bags, for example, should be rated for -20 °F to -40 °F (-29 °C to -40 °C). **Insulated** clothing, including base layers, wool socks, a parka, waterproof pants, a hat, a facemask, gloves, and boots, is necessary. Climbers will also need special protective eyewear known as glacier glasses, which are designed to provide full coverage against the glare off snow and ice as well as the ultraviolet rays from the sun.

Climbers will need to buy or rent equipment that will help keep them safe on the mountain. In addition to a variety of packs to carry clothing and equipment,

THE COST TO CLIMB

Mountain climbing can be a costly sport. In addition to all the technical equipment, clothing, and other gear, climbers often have to pay for permits to climb specific peaks as well as transportation and lodging. For climbers attempting to summit Mount Vinson, guided expeditions can cost between $45,000 and $50,000 per person. That doesn't included the cost of getting to the departure point in Chile, and it often doesn't cover personal equipment costs (some companies provide group gear, but others do not). Only Mount Everest, in Nepal, costs more to climb; the average cost per climber for Everest is almost $85,000.

ICE AXE AND CRAMPONS

every climber needs an ice axe, a climbing harness, several carabiners, trekking poles, and **crampons** to provide grip on the icy surface. Avalanche transceivers or beacons, which send signals to other transceivers and can help locate lost climbers, are recommended on Mount Vinson.

Once everything is packed, the next step is to get to Antarctica. Most trips to Mount Vinson start in Chile. Many climbers depart from the city of Punta Arenas, at the southern tip of Chile. Punta Arenas sits on the Strait of Magellan, which connects the Atlantic and Pacific oceans. It is only about 882 miles (1,419 km) from the coast of Antarctica. Many cruise ships bound for Antarctica depart from the Punta Arenas port. Charter flights to Antarctica—specifically to the Union Glacier camp—depart from Presidente Carlos Ibáñez del Campo International Airport.

Once at the Union Glacier camp, climbers must wait for favorable weather conditions to take a short flight to Base Camp, which is located on the western side of Branscomb Glacier. Base Camp sits in a narrow valley at approximately 7,000 feet (2,134 m). Although the summit itself isn't visible at any point along the route, climbers can see the last icy ridges leading to the peak from Base Camp.

Over the next few days, climbers **acclimatize** to the altitude and climate by carrying supplies in backpacks and on sleds to Low Camp, a distance of about 5.5 miles (9 km). Although the slope is gentle and the climbing relatively easy, **crevasses** can be a problem. As a precaution, groups often travel roped together throughout the duration of the climb. If a climber falls into one of the wedge-shaped cracks in the glacial ice, the ropes make for a much easier rescue.

Climbers can go glamping ("glamorous camping") at Three Glaciers Retreat before or after summiting Vinson.

LAYER BY LAYER

One of the most challenging parts of climbing Mount Vinson is preparing for the extreme weather conditions. Although temperatures are always cold, the bright sun and physical exertion can warm climbers up. That's why experienced mountaineers recommend dressing in layers—six on top and four on the bottom. The key is to pair lightweight layers with heavier layers and to choose insulating materials such as Merino wool, fleece, down, and synthetic fabrics. Layered gloves and mittens, as well as hoods, hats, and balaclavas or other facemasks, are also a necessity. The final layer on top provides a different type of protection: a certified climbing helmet.

The next stage goes up a 45-degree incline to High Camp. Weather becomes more tricky at this elevation, and guides often wait for a stable forecast to start upward. Once there, many groups set up their tents and stay sheltered for a day or more so that climbers can rest and acclimatize before working toward the summit.

From High Camp, the route goes up a steep, icy slope to the rocky summit. Only after crossing the final ridge do climbers finally see the peak. Once there, they also see the peaks of the rest of Vinson Massif, including Mount Gardner, Tyree, Epperly, and Shinn. After pausing to take it in, however, climbers must turn around and retrace their steps back to High Camp—a 9-mile (14-km) round trip that can take up to 12 hours to complete.

Most climbers ascend using this established "normal" route, and most groups use the established camps along the way. Other options exist, but they are more technically difficult. Climbers have approached the summit from the south and north. Reaching the summit from the eastern side of the mountain involves scaling a nearly vertical wall of ice. The first successful attempt from the east didn't occur until 2001.

Getting to the summit and back can take as few as four days if the weather is perfect. Most trips take between five and nine days to complete. Climbers may also have to wait for flights to come pick them up once they return to Base Camp. Most of the approximately 1,400 climbers who have reached the summit of Mount Vinson would say that the expansive view of Antarctica from the top makes any delays worth it.

ROALD AMUNDSEN

CHAPTER 4: SEEKING THE SUMMIT

Mount Vinson was the last of the Seven Summits to be discovered. It was also the last to be conquered by climbers. Two American scientists named Tom Bastien and John Splettstoesser had explored the Ellsworth Mountains in the early 1960s, but they did not attempt to climb Mount Vinson. It wasn't until December 18, 1966, that the first climbers reached its summit—more than 30 years after Ellsworth first spotted its range and almost 10 years after the peak was officially discovered in 1957.

Several mountaineering groups were eager to be the first to summit Mount Vinson, but no one had received official permission or the necessary financial backing to do so. Then, in the fall of 1966, the U.S. government reached out to Robert Bates, a well-known climber and a member of the American Alpine Club, and asked if it would be possible to mount an expedition before the end of the year. Bates called his friend Nicholas Clinch and asked him to lead it. Clinch put together a team of 10 experienced scientists and mountaineers,

Climbing steep snow-covered mountain slopes requires preparation, skill, and the proper equipment.

CONRAD ANKER

ICY DOCUMENTARY

The PBS science show *Nova* has created documentaries about mountaineering expeditions on several of the Seven Summits, including Mount Everest in Nepal and Denali in the U.S. state of Alaska. In 2001, the show decided to document the expedition led by Conrad Anker up the eastern side of Mount Vinson. The film crew battled winds up to 60 miles (97 km) per hour and temperatures below -35 °F (-37 °C). They lugged a high-definition camera that weighed 42 pounds (19 kg) as they navigated over ice blocks they described as "house-sized." The documentary originally aired on February 11, 2003, and it's still available to watch on YouTube.

Like the Vinson Massif, the Craddock Massif is also part of the Sentinel Range in the Ellsworth Mountains.

known as the American Antarctic Mountaineering Expedition (AAME), and started planning the climb.

By December 7, 1966, Clinch and his team—Barry Corbet, John Evans, Eiichi Fukushima, Charley Hollister, Bill Long, Brian Marts, Pete Schoening, Samuel Silverstein, and Richard Wahlstrom—had arrived at their first camp in Antarctica. They had more than 2,400 pounds (1,089 kg) of gear and a motorized toboggan to help haul it. The team's progress was hindered by a three-day storm that flattened their tents and scattered their supplies across the glacier. But once the storm passed, the team split into three groups and began the ascent to the final camp and then to the summit. The first group of four, led by Clinch, made it to Vinson's summit on December 18. A day later, the next group arrived. The final members of the team summited on December 20.

Their arrival at the peak of Mount Vinson marked the last "first" among the highest mountains on each continent. It would be more than a decade before another attempt was made. In 1979, Werner Buggisch, Peter von Gizycki, and Victor Samsonov, who were working with U.S. **geologists** near the Sentinel Range, set off on their own to reach the peak. Buggisch and von Gizycki were from Germany, and Samsonov from the Soviet Union. They had been told not to attempt any summits while participating in the scientific research on Antarctica. But they did it anyway. They reached the top of Mount Vinson on December 22, 1979. Samsonov left his ski pole at the summit—and it remained there until 2007.

Once Mount Vinson had been successfully summited, climbing enthusiasts started wondering if it would be possible to scale all Seven Summits. Doing so would require a great deal of funding and time, as well as tremendous skill and courage. The first person to accomplish the feat was Richard Bass, an American businessman who owned a ski resort in Utah and who was an avid mountain climber. Mount Vinson was one of six summits he reached in 1983; he completed the final climb, of Mount Everest, two years later, at the age of 55.

The early expeditions up Mount Vinson used what is now referred to as the normal or standard route on the western side of the mountain. Most climbing expeditions since then have followed roughly the same path

A false-color satellite image of the Vinson Massif highlights the sharp, steep slopes.

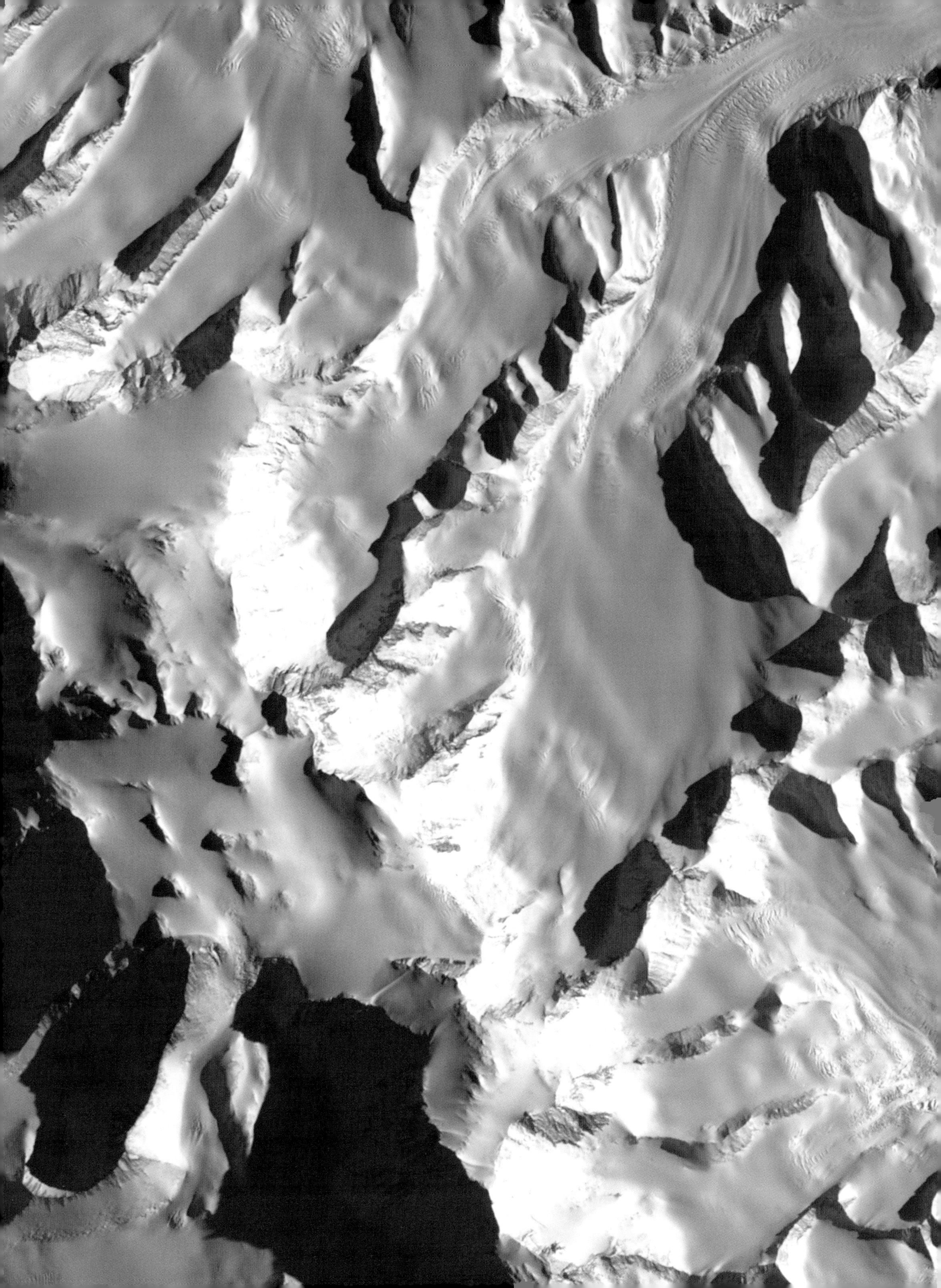

to the peak. But in 2001, a team of eight climbers led by Conrad Anker made the first successful climb up the eastern side. The trip was sponsored by *Nova*, an American Public Broadcasting Service (PBS) science program that wanted to do a documentary about the climb. In addition to the experienced climbers, including author and mountaineer Jon Krakauer, and scientists on the team, two camera

Explorer Roald Amundsen took this photo on an Antarctic expedition in the early 1910s.

Climber Satyarup Siddhanta reached the summit of Mount Everest in 2016.

operators and a producer were also along for the 17-day trip. The documentary they produced was called *Mountain of Ice*.

On December 15, 2017, an Indian mountaineer named Satyarup Siddhanta reached the summit of Mount Vinson. It was the last of the Seven Summits for him. A year later, Siddhanta completed the Seven Volcanic Summits, one on each continent. He was just 35 years old, which made him the youngest person to complete both lists. As a child, Siddhanta had struggled with asthma, a lung disease that can make it hard to breathe. He relied on inhalers to help regulate his breathing. Climbing was a challenge at first, but exercising helped him get stronger and to breathe easier without an inhaler.

In 2019, Arunima Sinha became the first female amputee to climb Mount Vinson. Sinha had lost her leg after being pushed out of a train in 2011 and decided during her recovery to climb Mount Everest. After accomplishing that feat in 2013, Sinha decided to climb each of the Seven Summits and plant the flag of her home country, India, on each of them. Mount Vinson was the final mountain in her quest. She reached the summit on January 4, 2019.

Today, there are several companies that offer guided expeditions up Mount Vinson, each with experienced climbers leading the tours. One of the most well-known guides to lead expeditions up Mount Vinson is Dave Hahn. Hahn has reached Vinson's summit 38 times—although he may be better known for summiting Mount Everest 15 times. Hahn has climbed Vinson from both the western and eastern sides, and he helped guide the film crew that produced *Mountain of Ice*.

Although exact numbers are not available, an estimated 1,400 people have climbed Mount Vinson. Despite challenging weather conditions, most climbers who are able to get to Antarctica to start the climb are also able to finish it. Whether they are climbing Mount Vinson to become part of the exclusive Seven Summits Club or just to experience the highest point in Antarctica, everyone who reaches the top has achieved a tremendous feat. And not only are they rewarded with a breathtaking view of the land surrounding the South Pole, they also know they've accomplished something only a tiny fraction of the world's population has been able to do.

STAYING ALIVE

Mountain climbing is a dangerous pursuit. The higher the mountain, the more dangerous it becomes. Mount Everest, the highest mountain on Earth, is also the most deadly mountain on Earth. As of 2022, 314 climbers had died while attempting to summit it. But as of early 2024, no climbing deaths had been recorded for Mount Vinson. That success rate is due in part to the almost 10,000-foot (3,048-m) difference in height. And despite the extreme weather conditions, Vinson is not technically difficult to climb. That said, it is still dangerous, from huge cracks in the ice and steep drops to plunging temperatures.

STORIES OF THE SUMMIT

NICHOLAS CLINCH

When Nicholas Clinch died in 2016 at the age of 85, the headline of his *New York Times* obituary said he "took on unclimbed mountains." Three times he led teams up mountains that had not yet been climbed: first in 1958, up Hidden Peak in Pakistan; then Mount Masherbrum, a peak sometimes called Doomsday Mountain, also in Pakistan, in 1960; and finally, in 1966, Mount Vinson in Antarctica.

Nicholas was not the typical mountain climber. He was a tall, thin lawyer who suffered from a lung disease called asthma. But he was smart and practical, and he never quit. He believed that mountains were great equalizers on which seasoned athletes and average climbers alike had to face the same challenges. "The mountains don't care who you are," he once said.

Although he was a serious climber, Nicholas had fun along the way, too. In one story about the Vinson trip, the team had somehow lost some critical supplies—including fuel for their motorized toboggan—in transit. Nicholas took a small group to try to find the missing supplies and returned just as the rest of the team was losing hope. One of his teammates later remembered seeing him riding the toboggan "cowboy-style" atop a barrel of fuel. Nicholas's success on Mount Vinson led to the naming of Clinch Peak in 2006. It's a 15,883-foot (4,841-m) mountain just 1.5 miles (2.4 km) from Vinson.

LIESL CLARK

Liesl Clark had already been on higher mountains by the time a Twin Otter plane dropped her on the eastern side of Mount Vinson as part of an eight-person team attempting a new route to the top. In her role as a producer for the PBS science show *Nova*, Clark had traveled to Mount Everest five times and had climbed as high as 24,000 feet (7,315 m). She had gone above 16,000 feet (4,877 m) on Mount Denali. But she had not gone all the way to the top of either Denali or Everest, or of any of the Seven Summits.

That changed during the Vinson expedition.

The route the crew took up Mount Vinson was new and more dangerous than the one climbers typically used. It included scaling a near-vertical wall of ice blocks. But with the help of guide Dave Hahn, Liesl and the camera crew navigated it safely. The next day, they set out for the summit. But Liesl woke with a pounding headache—a sure sign of **altitude sickness**. She tried to power through the pain but soon signaled that she couldn't continue. Her guide, however, would not let her quit. He convinced her to stick with him and get to the top. Although it took half an hour longer than the rest of the team, Liesl made it. And how did she react? "I was doing my best, between dry heaves, to appreciate the spectacular view," Liesl wrote.

GLOSSARY

acclimatize—to adjust or get used to a new environment

agility—the ability to move quickly and easily

altitude sickness—swelling of the lungs or brain caused by air pressure at high altitudes

cardiovascular—having to do with the heart

crampon—a metal plate with spikes attached to a boot for walking or climbing on rock or ice

crevasse—a deep crack in a glacier or other body of ice

geologist—a scientist who studies the history of Earth, particularly by examining rocks

global positioning system—GPS; a system of satellites, computers, and other electronic devices that work together to determine the location of objects or living things that carry a trackable device

indigenous—relating to the earliest known native inhabitants of a region

insulated—protected from the loss of heat

massif—a portion of a mountain range that contains one or more peaks

sedimentary—left behind by water, wind, or glaciers

Seven Summits—a group that includes the tallest mountain on each of the seven continents

supercontinent—a huge ancient landmass from which today's continents are thought to have broken off

tectonic plate—a huge, rocky piece of Earth's shell that slowly moves around the world, carrying the continents and the ocean floor with it

SELECTED BIBLIOGRAPHY

Arnette, Alan. "The Gear You Need to Hike Mt. Vinson." Outside. November 18, 2010. https://www.outsideonline.com/outdoor-gear/hiking-gear/mt-vinson-gear-discussion.

Bell, Steve, ed. *Seven Summits: The Quest to Reach the Highest Point on Every Continent.* Boston: Little, Brown, 2000.

Bisharat, Andrew. "Into the Teeth of an Antarctic Climbing Expedition." *National Geographic.* December 11, 2017. https://www.nationalgeographic.com/adventure/article/antarctic-climbing-expedition-plans-history.

Hamill, Mike. *Climbing the Seven Summits: A Comprehensive Guide to the Continents' Highest Peaks.* Seattle, Wash.: Mountaineers Books, 2012.

Schaeffer, David N. *Five Big Mountains: A Regular Guy's Guide to Climbing Orizaba, Elbrus, Kilimanjaro, Aconcagua, and Vinson.* Macon, Ga.: Mercer University Press: 2010.

Wood, Elizabeth. "Climbing Antarctica's Highest Mountain for Alzheimer's Society (Part Two)." Alzheimer's Society. February 14, 2018. https://www.alzheimers.org.uk/blog/climbing-antarcticas-highest-mountain-alzheimers-society-part-two.

WEBSITES

7 Summits Club

https://7summitsclub.com
Learn about the world's tallest peaks and the people who climb them.

Britannica

https://www.britannica.com/sports/mountaineering
Explore the sport of mountaineering, including history and techniques.

National Geographic

https://education.nationalgeographic.org/resource/mount-vinson
Discover facts about Mount Vinson.

INDEX